Dinner With Groucho

Born in Donegal, Frank McGuinness lives in Dublin and is Professor Emeritus in Creative Writing at University College Dublin. His plays include *The Factory Girls* (1982), *Baglady* (1985), *Observe the Sons of Ulster Marching Towards the Somme* (1985), *Innocence* (1986), *Carthaginians* (1988), *Mary and Lizzie* (1989), *The Bread Man* (1991), *Someone Who'll Watch Over Me* (1992), *The Bird Sanctuary* (1994), *Mutabilitie* (1997), *Dolly West's Kitchen* (1999), *Gates of Gold* (2002), *Speaking Like Magpies* (2005), *There Came a Gypsy Riding* (2007), *Greta Garbo Came to Donegal* (2010), *The Match Box* (2012), *The Hanging Gardens* (2013) and *The Visiting Hour* (2021). Among his many widely staged versions are *Rosmersholm* (1987), *Peer Gynt* (1988), *Hedda Gabler* (1994), *A Doll's House* (1997), *The Lady from the Sea* (2008), *Oedipus* (2008), *Helen* (2009), *Ghosts* (2010), *John Gabriel Borkman* (2010), *Damned by Despair* (2012) and *The Dead* (2012).

FRANK McGUINNESS

Dinner With Groucho

Best Wishes

Frank Mc Guinness

faber

First published in 2022
by Faber and Faber Limited
74–77 Great Russell Street
London WC1B 3DA

Typeset by Brighton Gray
Printed and bound in the UK by CPI Group (Ltd), Croydon CRO 4YY

A CIP record for this book
is available from the British Library

978-0-571-38096-1

MIX
Paper from
responsible sources
FSC® C013604

2 4 6 8 10 9 7 5 3 1

For Alison McKenna

Dinner With Groucho was first produced at The Civic, Dublin, on 27 September 2022, by b*spoke theatre company, with the following cast:

Groucho Ian Bartholomew
Proprietor Ingrid Craigie
Tom Greg Hicks

Director Loveday Ingram
Set Designer Adam Wiltshire
Costume Designer Joan Bergin
Costume Design Assistant Gabriel O'Brien
Lighting Designer Paul Keogan
Choreographer David Bolger
Composer & Sound Designer Conor Linehan
Production Manager Eamon Fox
Stage Manager Audrey Cepeda
Assistant Stage Manager Rachel Spratt
Assistant Stage Manager Abi Cepeda
Production Assistant Rachel Heyburn
Producer Alison McKenna

Characters

Groucho
a comedian

Tom
a writer

Proprietor
whatever she chooses to be

DINNER WITH GROUCHO

A small restaurant, perhaps not all that it seems.

There is sawdust on the floor, and scattered oyster shells.

There is only one table, quite sizeable, covered by a chequered cloth.

There is a kitchen in this restaurant but it should not be obvious where.

The Proprietor can appear and disappear as she pleases.

SCENE ONE: SOUP

Music, 'The Boy I Love is Up the Gallery', is playing very lowly, barely audible.

The Proprietor is alone in the empty restaurant.

The table at which Groucho and Tom will sit is already set for dinner and is dimly lit.

The Proprietor looks at the arrangement of cutlery and glasses.

She starts to move the glasses about the table until she is satisfied with where they stand.

This she does very carefully.

She could be simply putting the final touches to laying the table – or she could be starting a séance.

When she is finished, she stands by the table and whispers.

Proprietor Bones, rest quietly.

Earth, lie lightly.

But now – rise, rise –

She claps her hands twice.

A blast of music and flash of light that could blind.

In that flash of light Tom and Groucho sit at the table, finishing their soup.

Tom looks every inch the successful publisher, immaculate suit, white shirt, neat tie, sitting there with a large napkin tucked under his chin.

Groucho looks like Groucho.

Groucho It's good.

Tom Yes, it's chicken.

Groucho Chicken?

Tom Not duck.

Groucho Duck?

Tom Duck soup.

Groucho No, it's not.

They continue to drink the soup.

Tom I enjoyed that film.

Groucho Chicken soup?

Tom *Duck Soup* – you made it.

Groucho I made *Duck Soup*?

Tom Yes.

Groucho I never tasted it – I couldn't have.
I'm against ducks – they quack.
Anything that quacks isn't kosher.
That's in the Bible.
I enjoyed that book – have you read it?
Did you enjoy it – you enjoyed *Duck Soup*.
I'm glad – you're very handsome.

Tom Handsome?

Groucho A Yiddish word – can't be translated.

Tom Into English?

Groucho Swedish – Greta Garbo, she was handsome, she was Swedish, we wanted her for a movie.
She turned us down – it was in English, the movie.
She didn't want to play dumb, but I said, Greta, dumb is dumb, in English – in Swedish – so play dumbo, noooo, she says.
They'll love you, we'll love you, noooo, she says.
She went for O'Neill instead – that's Eugene O'Neill.
Mourning Becomes Electric, Desire Under the Elves, Long Day's Journey into Brooklyn – A Tree Grows – gimme a visky.

Tom You would like a whiskey?

Groucho The wine's fine – your health.

He toasts Tom.

Tom Your health.

Groucho No, your health.

Tom And your health.

Groucho No, no, I insist your health.

He downs the wine.

My health isn't great – not like this soup, it's great.

Tom What's wrong with it?

Groucho The soup? Nothing. It's perfect.

Tom Your health?

Groucho No, your health. Cheers.

He toasts Tom with an empty glass.

One of us is drinking too fast.

He eyeballs the glass.

One of us is drinking too fast?

Groucho conducts a conversation with his wine glass.

Yes, one of us is.
   Which one? You drank me.
   I drank you?
   I was filled to the brim, now I'm empty – you drank me.
   I think that is not the case.
   I am not a case of wine, I am a glass and you drank me
too fast.
   Hold it – hold it – you're going too fast for me.

Tom Would you like more wine?

Groucho Yes, that might shut this guy up – I thought you'd
never ask.
   You thought he'd never ask?
   Don't ask – just pour.

Tom pours Groucho wine.

Your health.

Tom My health?

Groucho Your health.

Tom My health.

Groucho This is good wine – good soup.

Tom I'm glad you're enjoying it.

Groucho I am.

Tom What is Greta Garbo like?

Groucho A duck.

Tom She quacks?

Groucho She does.

Tom I knew a girl who looked like her.
Or was it she too quacked like a duck?
And she lay eggs.
Or was she hatched from one?
Helen – was that her name?
I don't recall.
She lived in a street near me in St Louis.
I can't remember where exactly.

Groucho Place yourself back there –

Tom With great difficulty –

Groucho Did the street run parallel or perpendicular to where you lived?

Tom I think that it was both –

Groucho Parallel and perpendicular?
I like that.
No one knows where's where.
Parallel and perpendicular –

Tom Geometry is not my forte.
I often got lost in St Louis – it's why I had to leave it.
What brings you to London?

Groucho To see you, Mr Eliot.

Tom See me?

Groucho I told you in my letters – I so admire your writing –

Tom And I admire your films. So fast, so funny, so –

Groucho Shakespearian?

Tom Much faster – much funnier.
Spare me from his clowns.
He was not always right.
No one ever is, are they?
But you are certainly right about this soup.
Good soup – chicken soup.

Groucho Do you know how to make perfect chicken soup?

Tom Tell me.

Groucho Clean the chicken.
Place it in a deep pot.
Water.
Add onions, carrots, celery, parsnips, dill, salt, pepper –
and a secret ingredient.
Boil it, simmer it, strain, chill, skim off the fat – reheat.
Serve, with noodles if you like.
The question is –

Tom What is the secret ingredient?

Groucho Tell me.

Tom Sugar – an ample pinch of sugar.

Groucho Correct – how did you guess that?

Tom You let it slip – during the recipe.

Groucho I let it slip?

Tom People do.
    They always do.
    What they most want to hide.

Groucho Why sugar?

Tom Again and again the secret is sugar.
    Perpetually, consistently, eternally –

Groucho Are you a spy?

Tom That would be telling.

Groucho Telling what?

Tom My recipe.

Groucho For chicken soup?

Tom Duck soup.
    But you are the master in making that delicacy, aren't you?

Groucho You did enjoy that movie?

Tom It made me laugh – it made me think.

Groucho Think?

Tom I learned so much from it – very much.

Groucho What?

Tom You love the English language.

Groucho I do?

Tom Yes – how you struggle to say in so many words what
you don't mean.
    You have that gift.

Groucho Of words?

Tom Of struggle.
    More wine?

Groucho Yes.

Tom pours more wine for Groucho.

Tom I am honoured to meet you.
You are, as they say, a man after my own heart.
And you have lifted mine.
My heart, that is.
I owe you for this kindness – that gift.
Thank you.

Groucho quietly breaks down at this.
  Tom lets him weep a little, then gently reprimands him.

You are crying into your soup, sir.

Groucho I am honoured to meet you.

Tom Then we are doubly honoured.

Groucho stops weeping.
  He sips more wine.

Groucho I apologise.

Tom Do.

Groucho This is a nice restaurant.

Tom Excellent.

Groucho And sawdust on the floor.
A sawdust restaurant.

Tom Excellent sawdust.

Groucho You could draw patterns in it.

Tom I told you – geometry is beyond me.

Groucho Do you come here often?

Tom For lunch occasionally.

Groucho When it's empty?

Tom I prefer empty restaurants.

Groucho Why?

Tom Women don't faint at the sight of my handsome face.
Men don't weep when I honour them.

Groucho I have apologised – I was nervous.

Tom Why?

Groucho Meeting you.

Tom You've met me.

Groucho raises his glass.

Groucho Your health –

Tom My health, what of it?

Groucho Your health –

Tom I'm ailing.

Groucho I apologise.

Tom Why?
I am simply under the weather.
I blame the moon for that.
It has begun to affect me.
My body waxes and wanes.
Wanes – what an accurate word.
I see the moon, the moon sees me, and while the moon is shining, I am not disappointed with my life.
As you are.

Groucho Disappointed?

Tom Am I being too forward?
Too direct?
It is an American trait I try to curb.
And yet there's times I admire vulgarity – rudeness, if you like.
Don't you?
Maybe not anymore – certainly not with me.

Groucho I've never stopped being rude.

Tom Good – then you won't stop being funny.

Groucho You want me to make you laugh?

Tom Isn't that why we are together?

Groucho Would you say so?

Tom This is my dinner with Groucho?

Groucho Dinner with Groucho.

A night to remember, that time I met T. S. Eliot.

Did I ever tell you about the time I met Houdini?

It was a crowded theatre, Houdini asked the audience for a volunteer – I rushed onstage – I love escape acts.

Houdini was going to be pulled by a chain in his mouth to the roof of the theatre.

He asked me to examine his mouth – was there anything in it?

Pyorrhoea, I said.

Brought the house down.

Timing, pure timing.

That was in the days when people knew what pyorrhoea meant.

And you had to be there, I guess.

Tom I wasn't there.

Groucho I noticed, you had done a Houdini.

What did you make of him?

Tom He was a popular performer, and I have always envied those who could win popular acclaim.

I envy their effortless ease, affecting their audience deeply – doing next to nothing.

Groucho Connecting nothing with nothing –

Tom Simply being there, coming and going –

I wrote an essay once about Marie Lloyd – an English music hall artist – you call it vaudeville in America –

Groucho Our country –

Tom Sometimes.

Marie Lloyd could control – no, she could contact her audience –

Groucho Contact?

Tom When she emptied her handbag – it was as if she were rummaging through the contents of her life.

Her life, their lives, their wives, mothers – those they loved – those they had lost.

And her song – she sang –

Tom sings.

'My old man said follow the van
And don't dilly dally on the way.
Off went the van with my old man in it –
I ran behind with my old cock linnet.
I dillied, I dallied, dallied and dillied –'

The Proprietor appears.

Proprietor Mr Eliot, this is not a singing establishment.

Tom I am so sorry –

Proprietor I have had occasion to warn you before.

Tom I was merely bowing the knee to your own Marie Lloyd –

Proprietor My own – my very own Marie.

The Proprietor sings.

'The boy I love is up in the gallery,
The boy I love is looking down at me,
There he is, can't you see, waving his handkerchief,
As merry as a robin that sings on a tree.'

Tom and the Proprietor sing in chorus.

Tom *and* **Proprietor**
'Now if I were a duchess and had a lot of money,
I'd give it to the boy who's going to marry me,
But I haven't got a penny, so we'll live on love and kisses,
And be just as happy as the birds on the tree.

The boy I love is up in the gallery,
The boy I love is looking down at me,
There he is, can't you see, waving his handkerchief,
As merry as a robin that sings on a tree.'

Groucho applauds.
  Tom and the Proprietor bow together.

Proprietor The usual main course, Mr Eliot?
  Steak?

Tom Steak would be lovely, thank you.

Proprietor I've just returned from the Baltic States, Mr Eliot,
did I tell you?

Tom How was Latvia?

Proprietor Latvia was lovely.

Tom And Riga?

Proprietor Lovely.

Tom Estonia, Tallinn?

Proprietor Quite lovely.

Tom Lithuania?

Proprietor Lithuania was Lithuania.

Tom Quite.

Proprietor Parched I was, quite parched.
  I tell you, if you ever visit there, bring a kettle and a
suitable plug.
  The whole idea of a cup of tea is a mystery to them.
  Steak for two it shall be.

  The Proprietor turns to Groucho.

There's no need to stand.

Groucho I'm not standing.

Proprietor I noticed.

  The Proprietor goes.

Groucho Quite the great lady, isn't she – sorta like the
Queen Mother.

Tom No relation, I'm afraid – no blue blood.

Groucho That's how she will bring the steak – blue?

Tom I could not say.

Groucho She didn't ask.

Tom She never does – serves the meat as she chooses.
I don't complain.
We never do, Europeans.

Groucho You're American. From St Louis.

Tom Yes.
The Missouri – raised by that river – the making of me.
Quite untamed – that stretch of water.
Hidden depth and sudden shallows.
Not the easiest to manoeuvre.
In my blood, the old Missouri.
Wild, when it so chooses.
Yes, I'm from St Louis.

Groucho St Louis.

Groucho sings.

'Meet me in St Louis, Louis,
Meet me at the fair –
Don't tell me the sun is shining
Any place but there.'

Tom I don't know that melody.

Groucho Judy Garland sang it.

Tom What an extraordinary name – still, she is a singer.

Groucho Sorta like Stearns – Thomas Stearns Eliot.
Extraordinary name – still, you are a poet.

Tom Publisher – I'm also a publisher, Faber and Faber.
That's my occupation, publisher.

Groucho That's where I wrote to you –

Tom Thank you so much for your letters – you're a
wonderful correspondent.

Groucho Thank you for replying, and for the portrait – so handsome –

Tom You've read my poetry –

Groucho And your essays – the minor Elizabethan playwrights –

Tom Dante, my essay on Dante –

Groucho When I read their works, I appreciate how Shakespeare is so far ahead of the posse –

Tom Do you know that in universities my essay on Dante is torn out of my *Collected Essays* so often – students take a razor blade and slit it open –

He makes a move with his steak knife through his napkin, cutting it to tatters.

They disembowel the innards of the book so often.
Gut it so cleanly.
Show such expertise in the twisting of the blade.
Libraries have to order more copies –

Groucho Good for business, the publishing business –

Tom This anarchic violence delights us at Faber and Faber.

Groucho So they are pleased?

Tom They may even encourage such disgraceful behaviour.

Groucho I would never mess with those guys.

Tom You should never mess with me.

Groucho Quite a dab hand with the old steak knife.
Was that your nickname when the mob ruled St Louis?
Steak Knife Tommy?

Tom The expertise has come in useful.

Groucho When?

Tom In my dealings with other poets – particularly youngsters.
Fear – I find they thrive on it.

It brings out the worst in them.
And I encourage that.

Groucho Why?

Tom It's a living.
Racketeering – blackmail – arson – I'm a practising
Anglican.

Groucho You could quite convert me.

Tom Somehow I doubt that.
But I could show you fear in a fistful of knife.

*Tom drops the knife quietly and resumes his usual
demeanour.*
The Proprietor appears.

Proprietor Refresh my memory – it was two steaks, yes?

Groucho Yes.

Proprietor Well done, yes?

Groucho Overdone, mistress.

Proprietor I beg your pardon?
Did you say overdone?
Is that a reflection on my cookery?

Groucho I've not tasted it yet.

Proprietor No, you haven't – vegetables?

Groucho Yes.

Proprietor Potatoes?

Groucho They're vegetables.

Proprietor I beg your pardon?

Groucho Potatoes are vegetables.

Silence.

Proprietor I see.
Difficult.
Are you Germanic?

Groucho French – Alsace – Lorraine – my dad –

Proprietor I call that Germanic.
I know the region – their passion for entrails.
Preferably disembowelled.
So, I was right –
There's something of Vienna about you.
There is a clock museum in that city.
I can hear ticking inside you.
Perhaps it is your heart.
You have attractive eyes.
You're Jewish – you've seen suffering.
Don't worship suffering.
It's bad for the digestion.
Now, meat – meat.
Steaks, well done – am I right?

Groucho Aren't you always right?

Proprietor I must be – if you say so.
You are the customer.

Groucho Yes, I am.

Proprietor Don't forget it.
I knew a man once who did.
Forget his manners, that is.
He too was from Alsace Lorraine.
Ended up in a quiche.
Or was it an Alsatian?
Probably both.

The Proprietor exits.

Groucho Who is that woman?

Tom I've often asked myself that question – never answered it.
I'm glad you've come to see me.

Groucho Why?

Tom I'm waning – the steak is good here.

Groucho Champagne?

Tom There is no champagne –

Groucho I noticed. Shall I order champagne?

Tom Yes – yes – champagne.

Intense light in a blast.
  Sound of champagne bottles opening.
  Music.
  Tom and Groucho dance separately to the music and
end at opposite ends of the table to where they sat in Scene
One.

SCENE TWO: MEAT

There is an empty champagne bottle on the table.

Tom Well, we polished that off.

Groucho Didn't we?

Tom Enjoy it?

Groucho So much so I could have another.

Tom Shall I order another?

Groucho You're in a drinking mood?

Tom I'm thinking of you.

Groucho Me – in a drinking mood?
What are you trying to do, young man?
Get me sozzled?
Pry my shoe from my foot, pour the precious nectar of la belle France into its leather, put your sweet lips to its sole and drink the contents dry?
All eight gallons.
There could never be enough champagne to wrangle me into a compromising position.
I warn you, I am spoken for.
I am also spoken against.
Sinned against, if you wish to know.
More sinned against than sinning, though I say it myself – has that been said before?

Tom *King Lear.*

Groucho What do you think of it – *King Lear?*

Tom He should have drunk champagne – drowned in the stuff.
Revelled in its blessings.

Anointed himself in the darkness of its light.
Danced in the stillness of this temple.
Come home – come here, back to the Missouri.
Bathe in this river of champagne.

Groucho Why?

Tom That would have been the saving of him.

Groucho Is he saved – in the end is he saved?

Tom Well, he dies –

Groucho Not a minute too soon?

Tom Perhaps.

Groucho He brings it on himself.

Tom How?

Groucho The storm.

Tom The storm?

Groucho Sure, the storm.
  He brings it on himself.
  What age is he?
  Three score and ten.
  Seventy years old, out in all weathers, no coat, no hat,
no galoshes.
  Where does he think he's in?
  The Bronx?
  Pop into a deli to take shelter, grab a sandwich, loads
of mayo, layers of pastrami, cholesterol rocketing –

Tom King Lear had cholesterol?

Groucho His father died from it.
  His mother encouraged it.
  What a bunch they were – the senior Lears.
  And she kept telling her only son, you'll never come to
anything, Bernie.
  Everyone else called him Lear, but she called him Bernie –

Tom Why?

Groucho To annoy him – he hated the name Bernard,
or Bernie.

When his children were born, all female, one after another,
she kept asking him, Bernie, where's my grandson? Give me a
grandson, Bernard.

He did not oblige, so she took it out on his girls.

She dressed little Regan and cute Goneril up in Davy
Crockett outfits, pants, guns, hats with tails – the whole
caboodle.

Is it a wonder that pair turned out like they did?

Their grandmother had them shooting raccoons from the
day and hour she got her hands on those broads.

And she encouraged them, saying – see that raccoon, he's
your father, shoot him.

What hope had they?

They had no hope – neither had the youngest.

Tom Cordelia?

Groucho Cordelia – the great family secret.

She was a boy – born a boy – her father raised her as a
woman and for why?

To spite his mother.

You want a son and heir, he said to himself, well, my fine
lady, that is what you won't get – my boy will be a girl.

That was why he was so fond of her, and wanted rid of
that confused kid at the same time.

That scene where he divides the kingdom –

He is not as crazy as he seems.

That guy had to hide this big family scandal, and he does.

Tom Cordelia marries –

Groucho Who to?

Tom The King of France.

Groucho French – queer – perfect.

Parfait, monsieur, parfait – and how do I have proof?

Tom Tell me.

Groucho He never shows his face again after they are hitched.
How could he?
It would blow his cover.
And do you know who makes sure the King of France
never sets foot again on the soil of England?

Tom Lear's mother?

Groucho You got it in one, Tom. She went to Paris with her
grandson Cordelia.

Tom Whom she thought was her granddaughter –

Groucho Correct –
The grandmother smelt something about this new
husband – something she had an instinct about – not that he
was queer, no siree.
She just watched him at meal time.
She noticed something up.
She would – it reminded her of her own marriage.
What could it be?
She guessed the magic word.
Which was?

Tom Cholesterol?

Groucho Right again, Mr Eliot – you're a hell of a literary
critic.

Tom I know, but thank you.

Groucho The pleasure is all mine, sir.
Cholesterol it is.
If she killed her own husband, just for the hell of it, why not
remove another offending party and strike a double blow –

Tom Why a double blow?

Groucho Follow this.
She removed her first husband, the King of England – next,
she kills the King of France – isn't something obvious?
She wanted to exterminate all royal families, and why?

Tom Isn't it obvious?

Groucho You tell me, Tom.

Tom The woman was a Democrat – all her life she voted Democrat –

Groucho They loved her in Boston – that's why she's buried there.

Tom Did he visit her grave?

Groucho Who?

Tom Lear – Bernie?

Groucho Only to dance on it – to make sure she was dead.

Tom And was she?

Groucho She was.

Tom How did she die?

Groucho Isn't it obvious?

Tom Cholesterol?

Groucho Too predictable for that piece of work – too obvious.
　　Dancing – she died from dancing.
　　Dancing in the rain – singing in the rain – out in the
storm – out in all weathers.
　　No hat – no coat – no galoshes – like mother, like son.
　　A tragedy.

Tom I must reread the play.

Groucho Do – so must I.

Tom You do read Shakespeare?

Groucho Have you been listening to me?
　　Read him?
　　I wrote him, Mr Eliot.
　　Cigar?

Tom So you do smoke?

Groucho I do – and you?

Tom nods and takes a cigar.

I smoke on medical advice.

Tom Your doctor approves?

Groucho He likes me to smoke.

Tom Rather different to mine.

Groucho I smoke – I choke – I go to see him – he tells me to cough – I cough – he charges – what does he charge me?
Let me count the ways – should I include the second opinion?
While we're at it, add in the third.
What did it come to – can I remember? Yes, I can.
Eight thousand bucks.

Tom And is it worth it?

Groucho Worth what?

Tom The cigar?
The smoke?

Groucho What would you say?

Tom Yes, it's worth it –

Tom produces a cigar from behind Groucho's ear.

A good cigar.
But I do wish they would behave – cigars.
This unappealing habit of appearing wherever and whenever they like – the government should be issuing warnings against that shocking development.

He produces another cigar from behind Groucho's ear.

Groucho Who are you precisely, Mr Eliot – a Cuban agent in the pay of Fidel Castro?
Does the government know of that?

Tom produces a third cigar from Groucho's jacket pocket.

Tom These kinds of unforeseen circumstances can lead to heart attacks.

Groucho They can for sure.

Tom How does your heart fare, Groucho?
Is it sturdy – beating hale and healthy?
Or fragile?

*Tom produces an egg from within his cupped hands.
He gives it to Groucho.*

A delicate souvenir of our meeting.

Groucho I shall treasure it.

Tom It is odd what we treasure – memories –

Groucho Magic –

Tom They can indeed be magical, and that is where I have difficulty.
I am beginning to forget my memories.
So, will I lose my magic?

From his own pocket Tom produces a multicoloured silk handkerchief.

It brings tears to my eyes.

*He wipes his eyes.
He hands the handkerchief to Groucho.*

Another souvenir – put it in your pocket, it is quite clean.

Groucho places it in his jacket pocket.

You did not say you would treasure it.

Groucho Was I meant to?

Tom Yes – I shall take it back.

*Tom takes the handkerchief from Groucho's packet.
It grows and grows.
Groucho applauds.*

Groucho You are full of surprises, Mr Eliot.

Tom You flatter me, Mr Marx.

Groucho Not at all, Mr Eliot.

Tom Have I finished, do you think?

Groucho I doubt it.

Tom And I hope you may be right, but I have.
Finished, finished entirely.
My bag of tricks is empty.
The act is winding down.
You have seen all I can do – I hope you find it amusing.

Groucho Amusing, and vibrant.

Tom Vibrant, and delightful.

Groucho Delightful, and vivacious.

Tom Vivacious, and provocative.

Groucho Provocative – remarkable.

Tom Remarkable – resounding.

Groucho Resounding, and amusing.

Tom Amusing, but we've said that.

Groucho So we're finished?

Tom I think so.

Groucho Why so sure?

Tom I feel it – in my bones.

Groucho Feel what?

Tom The moon – in my bones – waning –

Groucho Waxing –

Tom It gives me visions –

Groucho Showing what?

Tom It tells me –

Groucho Telling what?

Tom I have done my bit.

Groucho Your bit for magic? For poetry? For St Louis? For America?

Tom For none of these things.

Groucho Then for what – done your bit for what?

Tom For silence – I have earned my right to silence.

Groucho Why silence?

Tom Silence – the last refuge of the guilty.

Groucho What are you guilty of?

Tom America – St Louis – poetry – magic – I stand accused by each and every one and I plead guilty.

Groucho I do not recognise the court.

Tom Why not?

Groucho I will not recognise a court that has me as its judge.

Tom Who says you are the judge?

Groucho Have you not pleaded guilty?

Tom Did I?

Groucho Have I not just heard you?

Tom My memory, it's going – did I just tell you so?

Groucho So you remember telling me?

Tom Yes, I believe I do.

Groucho So, your memory is not gone?

Tom Perhaps not.

Groucho Perhaps nothing – you have lied to this court.

Tom A court I do not recognise – a judge I do not recognise.

Groucho You do not recognise my face?

Tom I never forget a face.
In your case, I will not make an exception.

Groucho Have we not just met?

Tom So you tell me.

Groucho It's what I've told myself.
But I may be mistaken.
I suggest we better meet again.

Tom When?

Groucho Now?

Tom If you like.

Groucho Take it away, Mr Eliot.

Groucho shakes Tom's hand.

Tom Mr Marx –

Groucho How nice to meet –

Tom How swell –

Groucho Swell – you said swell?
I expected better.

Tom I expected stranger.

Groucho We did not get what we expected in each other.

Tom We did not.
Should that not have been what we might have expected?

Groucho I cannot say.

Tom I would not say.

Groucho Why not?

Tom That would ruin my defence.

Groucho Which is?

Tom Silence, as I've said.

Groucho As I heard.

Tom My silence.

Groucho And my own, would you not say?

Tom I could not say.

Groucho Try.

Tom Shall we meet again?

Tom shakes Groucho's hand.

Groucho Mr Eliot –

Tom We meet again –

Groucho It has been delightful –

Tom Dignified –

Groucho Disturbing.

Tom Disturbed.

Groucho Depraved.

Tom Disgusting.

Groucho I shall complain.

Tom Do.

Groucho I shall consult my lawyer.

Tom I *am* your lawyer.

Groucho I shall consult you.

Tom I shall consult myself.

Groucho And what do you advise?

Tom My professional advice?
You want –

Groucho Your professional advice – what is it?

Tom Chickens, Mr Marx – breed chickens.

From under the table, Tom brandishes a plastic chicken.

How can you go wrong with chickens?

Tell me – that egg I gave you earlier – do you still have it about your person?

Groucho searches for the egg.

Groucho It's gone.

Tom Not gone, sir, but grown – grown –

Tom raises the plastic chicken triumphantly.

Hatched into this healthy specimen of a bird.

Groucho You are a master of your craft.

Tom My act?

Groucho Your art.

Tom A dying art.

Groucho Flourishing in your hands.

Tom Unsteady hands.

Groucho takes Tom's hands.

Groucho Best of hands – blessed hands – hands that wrote –

Tom *King Lear*?

Tom withdraws his hands.

No, not quite – I know my limitations.

Groucho *The Waste Land*.

Tom One long grumble.

Groucho 'The Love Song of J. Alfred Prufrock'.

Tom A rag – a tatter – words in the wind.

Groucho The *Four Quartets*.

Tom Four too many.

Groucho *Murder in the Cathedral*.

Tom Butcher the bishop – shoot the saint – do it quickly.

Groucho I could go on.

Tom I wish you wouldn't.
A mug's game – poetry.
Stop please.

Groucho As you wish.

Groucho grabs the rubber chicken and uses it as a ventriloquist's dummy.

But what do you say?
I say I'm hungry – where's the food – where's that
Proprietor?
Where is that healthy specimen of a bird?

Groucho calls.

Conductress – Proprietor – miss – miss –

The Proprietor appears from the kitchen.

Proprietor I have a name, you know.
In fact, I have several.

Groucho Can I guess?
If I do, can we get more food?
Is it Rumplestillskin?

Proprietor No – nor is it Snow White or Rapunzel.

Groucho Cinderella?

Proprietor Marguerite actually – or one of the many versions
thereof.
Marguerite – the pearl, the daisy, the Michaelmas daisy.
Marguerite – La Dame aux camélias.
Perhaps not – I am not now nor have I ever been tubercular.
Marguerite, or Margaret.
Margaret, and am I grieving over all that is unleafing?
It is the blight man was born for.
It is Margaret you mourn for.
So, it is Marguerite or Margaret – choose.
Either is acceptable.

But not Maggie – never, never, never Maggie.

The last man who tried addressing me with that unfortunate familiarity came to a sticky end.

Suffice to say I put to excellent use my time spent in Alsace Lorraine, during the last war, disembowelling.

Do I make myself clear?

Groucho Indeed, sir.

Proprietor Madam is acceptable.

Groucho I'll remember.

Proprietor Try.

Now, food – you were complaining of slow service.

Let me check your order.

Albatross?

Groucho Albatross?

Proprietor Albatross.

Which one of you gentlemen ordered albatross?

I do hope it isn't you, Mr Eliot.

You know what distress that choice of entrée causes in the kitchen.

The chef, the poor chef, the stories he can tell of his innumerable and, indeed, interminable sea voyages.

Tom Madam, I have always believed you are the chef.

Proprietor Only when I am in the kitchen, and I trust you observe I am not there now, am I?

Still, who am I to say?

A learned man like yourself might persuade me otherwise.

Perhaps I am in both the restaurant and the kitchen.

Perhaps I am young as I am aged.

Perhaps I am neither.

Perhaps I am changeable as air, light as ether.

Perhaps I am on the earth, solid as a rock.

Perhaps I am in the sea, a creature of perpetual motion.

Perhaps you will devour me.

She turns to Groucho.

Crab?

Groucho Only once – in Pittsburgh.

Proprietor Did you order crab claws?

Groucho Claws – scuttling across –

Proprietor Fried – did you order fried –

Groucho Albatross?

Proprietor Fried?

Groucho In butter.

Proprietor With or without?

Groucho Without –

Proprietor Shells?

Groucho If I order without, may I keep the shells?

Proprietor Then it's with?

Groucho Are we still talking about crabs?

Proprietor I believe you ordered albatross.
Have you not just informed me you wished to eat albatross?
Now, you've changed your mind – you require crab?

Groucho I'll take either.

Proprietor I'm afraid you can't – we're out of both.
And oysters – before anyone asks.

Tom No crab?

Proprietor No, Mr Eliot – my apologies.

Groucho No albatross?

Proprietor Not in the kitchen, but I can do – I am told I can do a particularly accurate impersonation of that afflicted creature.

Tom Madam, you must reveal to us this extraordinary talent.

Proprietor I couldn't, Mr Eliot, I absolutely couldn't.
I would die – simply die rather than do that, Mr Eliot, in front of your guest.
Not even in front of your own eyes.
I cannot – cannot – cannot do what you say.
Please, don't ask me – it is not in my nature.
No – no – no – no – no.

Silence.

Well, what did you make of it?

Groucho What was it?

Proprietor My albatross.

Groucho That was your albatross?

Proprietor They are shy creatures, sir – that is what I was mimicking.
Their timidity – their reticence – their modesty.
Did you expect me to fly?

Tom I knew what you were doing.

Proprietor I would expect no less, Mr Eliot.
You have seen my Great Auk.

Tom Could I ever forget it?

Proprietor He cried, sir – this noble gentleman, this distinguished poet, he cried.
He wept for the Great Auk.
Shed tears of sorrow for that species.
Extinct, sir.
An extinct species – as we will be one day, will we not, Mr Eliot?
As we may even be now as we speak.
Who can tell for sure?
How can we be certain in our minds?
The mind, Mr Eliot, the poor mind.

Does it ever cease wondering?
Will it never tire?
What can it not conjure?
Even the dreams after death.
What is he, your beloved Dante, but a dreamer after death?
A connoisseur of the damned.

From her pocket she pulls out leaves of pages of Eliot's
essay on Dante and scatters them about the restaurant.

Look at them, descending like lost souls.
Words – words in the immortal wind, blown by the breath
of Dante.
Perhaps he too wanders now among the shades of hell.
Did he once see what he would become – as we all will
become.
Damned.
Mr Eliot, are we all damned?

Tom You are in bleak mood today, madam.

Proprietor How can I not be, sir?
Today, how can I not be?

Groucho Why?

Proprietor Because we have no crabs.
We have no albatross either.

Groucho And the Auk – the Great Auk?
Are you fresh out of Auk?

Proprietor Are you trying to be what is vulgarly referred
to as funny?
Maybe not – maybe you know more than my good self.
Know more than Mr Eliot.
Perhaps you can enlighten us where we may purchase
a Great Auk for your delectation.
Harrods Food Hall? – Selfridges? – a flesher's shop in
High Wycombe?
Do let me know.
Speak up – speak up – I am all ears.

No – not a word out of you.
Not a syllable – not a peep.
Why not – cat got your tongue?

Groucho miaows.

I don't have to take this from customers like yourself.
I don't come here to be insulted.

Groucho Where do you usually go?

Proprietor The Royal Albert Hall.
I shall never again expose myself to the Scottish Symphony
Orchestra.
Mahler, in kilts, played on the pipes.
How could the BBC permit the like?
A sight – a sound not to relish.

Tom You are too sensitive, madam.

Proprietor It is a curse, sir – a curse.
At such cacophony my ears bleed – my eyes bleed – every
orifice bleeds.

She turns to Groucho.

Steak – bloody?

Groucho I'm sorry?

Proprietor Would you like to order steak?
Rare – bloody – Americain – raw?

Groucho Steak – medium.

Proprietor Mr Eliot, steak?

Tom As always, that would be fine.

Proprietor Blue?

Groucho Depends on the bull – its mental condition.

Proprietor Bull?

Groucho How do you get blue steak from a happy bull?

Proprietor Send it to spend an evening with you.
You have my sympathy, Mr Eliot.

The Proprietor exits.

Groucho Who is that woman?

Tom As I've said, I've often asked myself that question –
she never answered it.

Groucho Who owns this restaurant?

Tom She does – I've always presumed she does.

Groucho She doesn't get many customers.

Tom Quite exclusive – prides herself on that – quite choosy
who she lets sit here.

Groucho How does she choose?

Tom We all share her sympathy with the Great Auk.

Groucho Extinct –

Tom Dead, yes – or dying – a dying species.
And the steak is good here – champagne?

Groucho There is no champagne.

Tom I noticed.
Champagne?

Groucho Yes, yes – champagne.
More champagne.

Blast of music and intense light.
Sound of champagne opening.
*Tom and Groucho dance on the table and again change
places at the table.*

There are two more empty champagne bottles.

Groucho Well, we polished them off.

Tom Didn't we?

Groucho Enjoy it?

Tom So much, I could have another.

Groucho Shall I order another?

Tom You're in a drinking mood?

Groucho No – I have had my fill.

Tom Good champagne though.

Groucho Excellent champagne.
  I recently drank a strange vintage.

Tom Where?

Groucho The state of Israel.

Tom I have a keen admiration for that country.
  The climate is good?

Groucho Excellent.
  And I drank their champagne – Jewish champagne.

Tom Did you admire it?

Groucho As much as you admire that country.

Tom Meaning –

Groucho Meaning whatever we care to say, we will believe that.

Tom I would hope to visit there.

Groucho I'll let them know – they'll roll out the red carpet. Why is the carpet red?

I know why – it doesn't show the blood, even when we fall.

Even the best of us can slip and fall when it comes to state occasions.

Tom We stumble – even the worst of us.

Groucho We make mistakes.

Tom Bad ones – terrible ones.

Groucho We fall –

Tom Inebriated with the sense of shame.

Groucho Are you ashamed?

Tom Me – why?

Groucho I asked the question.

Tom And I'll answer with silence.

Silence.

What does that make me – in law, what does that make me?

Silence.

Silence presumes I'm innocent of charges levelled against me.

If I should speak, I would incriminate myself.

But I'll break silence – I'll ask you a question – interrogate you as you might interrogate me.

So at the risk of repeating myself, I ask, why am I ashamed?

Groucho Can I answer that with another question?

Tom I have set the precedent – please do.

Groucho Would you drink champagne from the state of Israel?

Tom That would depend.

Groucho On what?

Tom Not on what, but on who.
Who was pouring.
If it were you, I would drink it down, sitting in a dive
somewhere, in meanest Europe – Brussels or Antwerp –

Groucho Why?

Tom Do you not admire Jewish champagne – did you not
admit that?

Groucho Did you not admit you admired Israel?

Tom Then we each have made our admissions.
Well, at least I have, as far as I'm concerned.
And I will admit no more.
The subject is closed.

Groucho I will roll up the red carpet.

Tom Do – put it away.
One of us may fall and do ourselves damage.
Who would then repair us – our handsome faces?
Why do you keep sending me portraits?

Groucho So you'd recognise me.

Tom How could I not?

Groucho You do me a disservice – that could easily happen.
I am a master of disguise.
It is part of my mission – I must travel under cover.

Tom Tonight what is your mission?
Are you another spy for Fidel Castro?
Or is it the state of Israel?

Groucho I must travel under cover.

Tom What cover do you now assume?

Groucho You mean you haven't guessed?
These features – these fine features – this head – this
handsome head – the aura that surrounds me.
How well I've cultivated that aura.

Everyone who sees me – they gasp in wonder.
Don't you know who I am?

Tom You must tell me.

Groucho Tonight I am the poet, the distinguished man
of letters, T. S. Eliot.

Tom Delighted to meet you.

Groucho The delight is all mine.

Tom I cannot return the compliment.
I would never aspire to be Mr Groucho Marx.
And I'm afraid the conversation between myself and
myself will not be a productive one.

Groucho Are you telling me you never talk to yourself?

Tom Only during the most violent of quarrels, and I try
never to engage in such loutish behaviour.

Groucho Yet I put you down as a fighter – a boxer – the
champion of the world.

Tom You flatter me again, sir.
I only ever box with shadows, and the shadows inevitably
win.

Groucho Do you let them?

Tom I said they inevitably win – invariably win.

Groucho Why?

Tom Exhaustion?
Yes, I'll put it down to exhaustion.

Groucho What has tired you out?

Tom My life, I must presume.
It has wearied me, worn me down – yet I am cut from
hard stuff.
Hard as a brick, hard as the man who fathered me.
A model of fixed certainties, and of most rigorous dietary
laws.

He would not have sampled Jewish champagne, nor had it in his house.

I can be sure of that.

Groucho He didn't know what he was missing.

You could have told him that.

Crack open the champagne of beautiful Jerusalem –

Tom My father never cracked.

Well, not until he chose to.

It was then and only then I recognised something strange about him.

He was a man too frequently on the verge of weeping.

My father towards the end.

As yours, I imagine, was always on the verge of laughter.

Groucho My mother drowned him out, and why?

It might have interrupted her sons.

So my father – he did not get much of a look-in either way, laughing – weeping.

Tom You sprang from their loins –

Groucho You make me sound like a kangaroo –

Tom The funniest man in movies –

Groucho A family of kangaroos, breeding like rabbits –

Tom The funniest man in the world –

Groucho Now that would be funny – rabbits the size of roos taking over Australia, and not stopping there.

They'd hop to America – New York is their target.

One wallop of their scuts, the Statue of Liberty is gone.

Instead of that almighty dame, they erect a monument to the god of rabbits.

Where do they build it?

Where else but Coney Island?

And we will start to speak in high-pitch tones in homage to Bugs Bunny.

I really hate that buck-toothed guy.

I'm with Elmer Fudd – shoot the wabbit – please, shoot the wabbit.

Tom Consider him shot.

Groucho Thank you, Mr Fudd.

Tom I am now a cartoon character?

Groucho If it should please you –

Tom Why should it not?
That most fastidious of poets, Marianne Moore – I do admire her eloquence –

Groucho Why?

Tom Her accuracy.
Marianne Moore was a connoisseur of cartoons.
I may be wrong, but I believe her favourite was Sylvester the Cat.

Groucho Why?

Tom Because he failed – he always failed.
An exacting woman, Miss Moore.
As with all exacting people, she enjoyed courting failure.
Enjoyed spotting danger – no, creating danger, when she felt like it – getting out alive.
An escape act.
Like myself, she took refuge in silence, should that suit her mood.
Her finest poem –

Groucho quotes in its entirety Marianne Moore's poem, 'Silence':

Groucho
'My father used to say,
"Superior people never make long visits,
have to be shown Longfellow's grave
or the glass flowers at Harvard.
Self-reliant like the cat –

that takes its prey to privacy,
the mouse's limp tail hanging like a shoelace from
    its mouth –
they sometimes enjoy solitude,
and can be robbed of speech
by speech which has delighted them.
The deepest feeling always shows itself in silence;
not in silence, but restraint."
Nor was he insincere in saying, "Make my house
    your inn."
Inns are not residences.'

At the poem's conclusion, Tom applauds.

Tom I am speaking to the converted.

Groucho But do you think she could do one of my routines?

Tom Perhaps –

Groucho Baloney – that lady never played New Jersey.

Tom Not to my knowledge, but wonders never cease –
I shall enquire when next I see her.
    May I be so bold as to ask why you know that poem by
heart?

Groucho It's the story of my life.

Tom A tragic story –

Groucho For a funny guy, you mean?
    Spotting danger – creating danger – getting out alive.
    Flying by the seat of my pants.
    Escaping by the skin of my teeth.
    Houdini – pure Houdini.

Tom Skin of one's teeth – seat of one's pants – all mouth and
buttocks.
    Flesh and enamel.
    Poetry – pure poetry.
    The enviable capacity to sing sweetly through our arses.
    Perfumed and putrid at one and the same time.

For this we are beloved.
Some are even revered.

Groucho Poets?

Tom You share our instincts.

Groucho I do?

Tom A mug's game, didn't I tell you?
We can make them believe anything.
We can sell anything.

Groucho I don't buy that.

Tom Neither do I.

Groucho Why say it then?

Tom Defiance, Groucho.
Innocent, insane defiance.
Reason gone mad.
What you call –

Groucho Comedy, Mr Eliot – pure comedy.

Tom And tragedy?

Groucho Paying the bill, sir – that is tragedy, the bill.
Which reminds me – this is my shout.

Tom I must insist –

Groucho You may insist, but I will pay – my pleasure,
my privilege.
Next time, you are host.

Tom I should be this time – I did choose the restaurant –

Groucho I will never forget it – the food, the company,
the service – the lack of it – where is she?

Tom Shall I call for her?

Groucho No point – I think she just appears when she's
required –

Tom Moving in mysterious ways?

45

Groucho No – that's the Staten Island Ferry.

Groucho calls out.

Madam?

The Proprietor appears.

Proprietor I am not deaf – there is no necessity to disturb the peace.
　The other customers will complain.

Groucho There are no other customers.

Proprietor That is a matter of opinion.
　I am run off my feet.
　You have been so engrossed in your discussions, the world has ceased turning as far as you two are concerned.
　Males, sitting there, elaborating on the ins and outs of existence, weighing the pros and cons of life, wondering is it worth persisting?
Am I not right – to be or not to be, and all that piffle?

Tom Piffle?

Proprietor Piffle, I said.
　To be or not to be – I have brooded on such mysteries.
　I have come to a conclusion.
　You do admire the Shakespeare chap, don't you?
　I am here to tell you he got the wrong question.
　That is not it at all.
　To be or not to be does not determine our lives.
　The line should be rewritten thus – to be is not to be.
　Death in life, life in death – to be is not to be, and this is the truth, gentlemen.
　We are both alive and dead, each and every one of us.
　Being and not being, at one and the same time.
　Our past is our present is our future.
　We are what we were, and what we will be.
　Ever there, ever changing, never staying the same.
　Bounce the ball of our existence.
　Follow where it may lead.

46

Follow fearlessly, and find a way through that confusion –
the muddle and the mess and the margins of where we are.

Confusions – contradictions – lovely labyrinths, at the root
of our lives.

Find them.

I know this as sure as my name is whatever you choose my
name to be.

It is knowledge which allows us to continue.

Continue as a species, man-woman, woman-man.

Well, it allows me to continue.

I will not commit suicide.

I must not commit suicide.

Groucho Good, it ruins the carpet.
Even the red one.

Proprietor The steaks – how were your steaks?

Groucho Tough – like my grandmother.
Tough as a Cossack's boot.
She adored the Cossacks.
She catered their pogroms, never got paid – not once.
She kept on doing it – every time.
She never committed suicide ever.
And she was in the catering business – do we ever learn?

Groucho takes the Proprietor's hand.

Proprietor We provide for bar mitzvahs.

Groucho I'll bear it in mind.

Proprietor Mr Eliot, are you doing the honours?

Tom My friend here insists –

She turns to Groucho.

Proprietor Poor you.

She is about to hand Groucho the bill.

I will have you know I do not expect gratuities, but I have
never complained about Mr Eliot.

Groucho So he's generous?

Proprietor He is accurate.

Groucho has a quick look at the bill and does a double take.

Is there a problem?

Groucho I don't follow –

Proprietor Follow – what is your carp now?

Groucho Swan?

Proprietor Yes?

Groucho Neither of us had swan.

Proprietor No?

Groucho Godwit.

Proprietor Godwit?

Groucho I don't even know what godwit is.

Tom A bird of the plover family – long, slightly upcurved bill –

Proprietor Long, slender legs, a great part of the tibia bare. Delicious, aren't they, Mr Eliot?

Tom I'm afraid I wouldn't know – I've never tasted it.

Groucho I also do not know what a shoveller is, but according to this, it's part of my bill.
Partridge, owl, cuckoo, ringdoves –

The Proprietor consults the bill.

Proprietor Pullets, duckling, teal, peacocks, rabbits, leverets –

Groucho And one thousand three hundred eggs, three great lobsters, two hundred prawns, salmon –

Proprietor Salt fish, dory, tench –

Groucho Mutton and lamb dowsets, and last but not least, my old favourite, neats' tongues and sweetbreads.

Proprietor I do apologise – I must have confused your order with another table.

Groucho There is no other table.

Proprietor These are tough times in catering.
  Must I be pilloried for elaborating a little on your bill of fare?
  Business is business, sir.
  I appeal to you, Mr Eliot – be my witness.
  Sometimes a little creativity with the truth is necessary in order to survive.

  She turns to Groucho.

I presume you are going to quarrel with the drinks bill?

Groucho You mean will I question whether we drank twenty-eight barrels of beer and four hundred gallons of wine?

Proprietor A slip of the pen.

Tom We did have champagne – three bottles.

Proprietor Thank you, Mr Eliot – I can rely on your honesty.
  This gentleman sees fit to call mine into question.
  These minor additions –

Groucho Let me continue.
  Dessert – figs, dates, prunes, currants, strawberries, gooseberries, cherries, pears, apples, damsons, oranges, quince –

Proprietor I distinctly heard someone order fresh fruit salad.

Groucho You did not hear us.

Proprietor Then who was it – a ghost?

Tom It may have been, my dear – you are so susceptible –

Proprietor And you are too kind, Mr Eliot, but as for your dining companion –

Tom This is Mr Marx, Groucho Marx –

Proprietor He could be the man in the moon for all I care.
Names do not impress me.

I have had the highest in the land and the salt of the earth
eat in my restaurant.

No one – no one has ever taken issue with what I say they
owe.

This is a first, Mr Eliot – a first –

Tom No, it is not, madam.

Proprietor It isn't?

Tom I'm afraid not – it happens every time.

Swans, godwits, cuckoos, leverets – does the list not sound
familiar?

Proprietor A little.

Tom You are confusing our meal with the bill of fare served
by the Merchant Taylors' Company to welcome Prince Henry
in 1607 –

Proprietor This has occurred before?

I've presented these charges to you before?

Tom Frequently.

Proprietor I do apologise for this error – quite unpardonable –

Tom On the contrary –

Proprietor I would not dream of putting you to such expense.

The Merchant Taylors' Company itself must bear the
expense of such a feast.

Tom Indeed they must.

Proprietor I will simply charge you for the soup – the
steaks – the champagne –

Tom Do.

Groucho puts a pile of notes on the table.

Groucho I don't know what's what in British money, but this
should cover it.

The Proprietor counts the notes.

Proprietor It will indeed – forgive my error.

Groucho Forgiven.

Proprietor You have the eyes of someone whose name
I cannot place.
I remember now.
James the First of England, Sixth of Scotland, father to
poor doomed Prince Harry.
How we lamented that dead child, Mr Eliot.
Myself and his Majesty.
They say in later years he looked completely mad.

She looks at Groucho.

Are you?

Groucho I well may be.

Proprietor It is why you have such compassion.
For our species.
Why you make us laugh.
You have compassion, yes.

Groucho I do?

Proprietor Indeed, as does Mr Eliot.

Groucho And he is also mad?

Proprietor As a March hare – why else would he dine here?
Why else would anyone eat in this establishment?

Groucho The service?

Proprietor My, how charming.

Tom Isn't he, my dear?

Proprietor Do call in when you pass this way again.

Groucho I would not miss it for the world.

Proprietor Don't say that – he shouldn't, should he,
Mr Eliot?

The world is much more to be cherished than that – isn't it, my dear?

What we were –

Tom What we are –

Proprietor What we will be.

Tom Our past is –

Proprietor Our present is –

Tom Our future.

Proprietor What have we but this world?

Tom Nothing.

Proprietor Nothing.

Groucho I can connect nothing with nothing.

Silence.

On Margate Sands –

Proprietor I have never been to Margate.
If you say I have, I deny everything.
Gentlemen, have you not got homes to haunt?
Be gone, be gone.
'Tis nearly midnight – the pumpkin hour – did you not call me Cinderella?
My beauty sleep, my dears.
My beauty sleep, my dears.

Groucho But it's dark outside –

Proprietor It will grow light –

Groucho Will you drive us into the night?

Proprietor You are creatures of the night, sir.
Does he not know this, Mr Eliot?

Groucho Know what?

Proprietor That you can return.

Tom Come and go.

Proprietor When you so wish – come and go.
Call as you please.

Tom But you, my dear, call us, don't you?

Proprietor I suppose I do.

Tom I've asked before – I'll ask again – why?

Proprietor Because you so enjoy it.
If you didn't, you wouldn't answer.
And it's proof in a way, isn't it?

Groucho Proof of what?

Proprietor That we survive.

Groucho Survive what?

Proprietor The cold – the cold that's coming.

Groucho How do we survive that?

Proprietor Champagne – drink champagne – champagne.
Drink and be gone.

Tom We go – we go –

Proprietor Be gone –

Champagne bottles explode, as does most of the restaurant in flashing light and noise.
Groucho and Tom disappear.
The Proprietor is left alone in the dim light that opened the play, holding a champagne bottle.

Come and go – gone again – probably taken the tip with them.
Bloody Americans.
Come again – do come and go – come.

Dropping the champagne bottle, like an epileptic, her body jerks and she speaks in a deep voice.

On Margate Sands I can connect nothing with nothing.

Silence.
    She recovers her normal voice.

Who is there – speak up – is that you, Mr Eliot?
    I am tired, my dear – worn to a frazzle – no more.

*She claps her hands, the lights dim further, isolating her in
the kitchen.*

Am I too turning into shadows?
    No – not yet – not extinct yet.
    Soon – soon.
    All be there soon.
    All be there soon.
    Bones, rest quietly.
    Earth, lie lightly.
    Then rise.
    Soon – soon.

She bows to her audience in the darkness.